Soul Ascension

A Journey of Insights

By

Elm Valle

DEDICATION

To Those I was privileged enough to cross paths with, and whom added color to my life. Without you, and the experiences you gave me, I would be incomplete. And to my wonderful daughters, Julianna & Ashlyn.

ACKNOWLEDGMENTS

God.
Family.
Friends.
Country.
Life.

Soul Ascension

A Journey of Insights

By
Elm Valle

A Journey of Insights

Table of Contents

A Journey of Insights

"Life is not measured by the number of breaths we take, but by the moments that take our breath away."

--Unknown--

A Journey of Insights

ഐ∾

Forethought

I wrote the first draft of this book almost two decades ago in 1999. Since then, many things happened in my life; some for the better, and some for the worse. Similarly, the world around me has also changed drastically. It is now the year 2016, and as I look back at the original words written in these pages; I am compelled to change this book as well (and I think to myself, wow, I am a terrible writer). Even our very thoughts, our soul, and our essence is malleable to the winds of change. As sure as the sun will continue to rise, the world with us in it, will continue to change. But this very fact is what makes each of our journeys unique and colorful.

Even before the advent of Philosophy, I am certain that our ancestors contemplated on the meaning of life. Why are we really here? What is my significance? Why me? These are tough questions in themselves. To add to the confusion, throw in cosmic change and the constant struggles we experience; then these questions all become but impossible to answer. With increased terrorism, global conflicts, and dwindling natural resources, it seems that 'hope' has become a buzzword used in political campaigns and marketing schemes trying to sell me something. Though that may be the immediate fact, the fundamental truth is that many of us would blame the society in which we live in. We seek ways to improve society and the external factors around us. But in order to do that, we must first look inward and contemplate on own lives. We as a species, are lost within our own storm. We do not take the time to truly understand the beauty of life and the importance of simply being.

The heartbreaking reality is, that there are many wrong and unjust matters in this world, especially in this generation. At some point, we all feel trapped, lost, and disillusioned. We all seek direction to help us understand our place in the world. We look to philosophy in the hopes it might guides us to the right paths. We are searching for even one candle in the dark that can light the way. Turning to history, our forefathers may have had the healthy ideology of living. They were simple in nature, yet complex in thinking.

Their creative powers brought forth the many luxuries found today.

Sadly, there is a part of this world that people choose to ignore and not experience. This overlooked world is full of wonders, derived from magic, dreams, and a breathtaking reality. Magic, fantasy, and dreams, are just labels given to ideas by people who do not understand the magnificence of the world. Some have experienced this splendor, and yet still refuse to believe possibilities of unrealized dreams. The lucky ones who are touched by these enchantments are inspired seemingly excel in almost everything. This is because success no longer become a priority, but instead, celebrate life under the contentment of simple existence. These people have the capacity to appreciate the humble simplicity found in nature. They are no longer burdened by insignificant trappings and accouterments of materiality or superficiality. Martin Luther King, Jr., Mahatma Gandhi, Confucius, John F. Kennedy, and Mother Teresa; all have reached a level of enlightenment; achieved only by shedding our society's preconceived definitions of success. Their motivation was not to achieve self-prominence but to grant greatness onto others through empathy, kindness, and sacrifice. Personally, I know I will never achieve their feats of greatness, but I do know that the actions I take today will be written into eternity. All of my actions, will define who I am; and especially through my children; and more so through the memories of those who I have affected.

I once thought the world cannot be changed by our own actions; that our contributions are insignificant. I was both right and wrong! The simple truth is that we cannot change the world we live in; because it is not the world that needs changing. We need to change the way we think and perceive the world. That change starts with you and I. And by changing the way we perceive and interact with the world around us, the world will change on its own. Every little word we say to someone, affects them and their actions. And in turn, that someone will affect another; and so forth and so forth. Soon the world begins to shift; unfortunately, it can change for the better or for the worse. So in this, we must place caution in how we affect others around us.

"You must be the change you wish to see in the world (Mahatma Gandhi)." In essence to change the world, you must first change. And in order to change we need to understand our most inner essence: our desires, fears, strengths, and joys. By bettering ourselves we can influence the rest of the world to follow. Be the stillness in the storm and soon others will gather to seek solace in your presence.

I do want to make clear though, that I will never claim to have the right answers or am I perfect in anyway. This book is simply my personal insights and lessons that I have learned through the years. I will try to unveil opportunities and possibilities that are often missed but have always been there. Most likely, you will not find the answers you are looking for in these pages. Hopefully you what you learn is of personal account and significance. This knowledge is priceless, because it is the key to understanding on how you interact with the world. As in life itself, I do not offer any guarantees that you will become a better person by reading this book; but hopefully it will provide you an atlas during your journey. Furthermore, the words within this book are simply what they are - words. Do not take them as solemn scripture, but do reflect on them under deep consideration. The ideas I have placed in this book may seem formless and shifting, but remember that the whole is the sum of its parts. An acute view of the universe will prevent you from uncovering the true beauty of what lies within it: the stars, the moon, the heavens, the ocean, and even a raindrop. In settled staid we lose the inner child in us, and that is the greatest tragedy. It is in the eyes of a child that views the world in prodigious manner that adults have long forgotten. In a child's eyes, opportunity is only bound by imagination. With that though, sit back, relax, and simply read this book. What you learn within these pages is bound only by your imagination.

CHAPTER ONE

Ripples in a Pond

"Never say there is nothing beautiful in the world anymore.
There is always something to make you wonder, in the shape
of a leaf, the trembling of a tree."
--Albert Schweitzer

When I was growing up in Italy, my brothers and I would throw pebbles into the nearby pond by the apartment complex where we lived in. Those pebbles would create ripples in the water, and the more pebbles we threw in the water, the more ripples would disturb the surface. When we stopped for a moment to catch a breath, the water would reflect the blue sky like a looking glass for the heavens. That serene surface would only last a few seconds, only to be broken by three pebbles that created three separate ripples. Back then, I really had no understanding of the significance of those ripples. Now, I know that those ripples represented our individual actions and how they can outwardly affect and spread to our surroundings. Those ripples represented how things begin and how nothing happens without action. They also show us how every action in life can affect another. As one pebble begins a series of ripples, so does another and eventually two ripples meet at some point, and thus change occurs within the surface of the water. Why is this of any significance? The individual ripples colliding and affecting each other demonstrates that our own actions are never without consequence. More importantly, our personal journey affects everyone around us; whether we perceive it or not.

To achieve and aspire greatness, one must turn thoughts into action. Action is the foundation of achievement. A single action, no matter how insignificant, can define the beginning of a journey. The challenge for most people, including myself, is taking that first step into uncertainty. Why is this first step so elusive? The answer is quite simple. We need inspiration to ignite us and motivation to propel us continually forward. This holds true even in our daily lives. So the question remains; how do we find that motivation, that spark, or that courage that can bring life into our own dreams and imaginations? The answer will be different for each and one of us. As children, we are easily inspired by the simplest things, but as adults we become unaware of those same exact things. We must learn to reopen our eyes and hearts again to the inspiration that already encircles us every single day. Inspiration is the flame that fuels the great minds of scientists, artists, musicians, and writers. Inspiration drives the creativity of the young and perpetuates the ideals of our elders. It is like a seed that grows into a tree with many branches; and with each branch reaching out to touch the far ends of the universe. The essence of inspiration can be found anywhere: from the leisurely fall of winter's first snow, to the resounding crash of the sea, and even in the gentle sighs of the wind. Inspiration starts like a stone dropped in a pond. Once that stone is released into the pond, it creates ripples. Eventually that ripple will touch every part of the pond. Inspiration certainly has humble beginnings but if we harness and nurture it; it can flourish into greatness. Through inspiration and dreams, ideas are born. Ideas, either positive or negative, perpetuate change in the direction of its essence. If you want to begin your journey, you must find your own inspiration in life. Remember, there is no such thing as a small dream. Let your inspirations become your motivation!

The real question you must ask yourself is not how to begin but whether you are ready to take the first step. Are you ready to begin? If the answer is yes, then you have already taken the first step into your own personal journey. The great thinkers of our generation knew that in order to change the world, they first had to change themselves. But they too had to take their 'first step'. Throughout the history of mankind, there is one word that allowed us to achieve great things: *Possibility.* To believe in possibility is to embrace inspiration, challenge convention, and to dream beyond the known.

At one point it was a fact that the Earth was flat. Then it was said we could never fly. Then we thought it would be impossible to reach the Moon. We also never knew the existence of molecules. All these things were at one point, deemed impossible but yet today they are common and trivial. There is that old adage: "We don't know what we don't know." In other words, the knowledge we know today may not be the knowledge for tomorrow.

We all must cast our own pebbles into the pond of life; whether it is a journey to change oneself or a journey to start something new. Inspiration is indeed a rare and special jewel. It is like a refreshing breath of air that suddenly fills your lungs. It is unfortunate that even though the world is filled with inspirations, we rarely take the time to look for them. Inspiration can be found in everything around us. Inspiration can even be found in anger, just as long as the energy of anger is released wisely. The greatest inspirer of things in nature is love. Look back upon your life and remember a time when you first fell in love with that special someone. Your love easily inspired poetry on paper and words in a song. If you still cannot find inspiration in yourself look to others. There is magic to be found everywhere; if a child can see this why can't we. Remember that the ripples in the pond we create, is our journey, and it has a profound and significant effect on others; whether we like it or not.

"To be properly expressed a thing must proceed from within, moved by its form." --Meister Eckhart

A Journey of Insights

CHAPTER TWO

Setting Sail

"In creating, the only hard thing's to begin."
--James Russell Lowell

As I grow older, I realize that it gets more difficult to start new endeavors. Maybe it is the old age setting in, or maybe it's the energy of youth leaving me. For whatever reason, I tend to choose things because it is safer, more comfortable, more familiar, and by doing so, I also realize I may be missing out on life's limitless continuity. I always wanted to write a book like this, but always convinced myself that I had neither time nor the energy. I had excuses not to write, until finally one day I decided to just write. What I eventually realized is, the first step to begin any journey is the most difficult one; but it is also the easiest one. Such a contradictory statement yet so true! I also look back in my own lifetime, and often wonder why I *did not* do something when I was younger. An important lesson I have learned is that there is no such thing as "too late."

Every moment of our lives is the beginning of the next moment. Thus in essence time offers us limitless opportunities to set forth on a task. Too often we tend to delay what we want to do. Soon that procrastination becomes our own undoing. Sometimes all we need is a small push in the right direction. Our minds are like rocks on top of a mountain with great potential. Once a rock is pushed down the mountain, it can catalyze a chain reaction that can become a landslide. On the other hand, sometimes we need more than just a small nudge, we need constant reminder. Regardless, accepting failure might be an outcome, is not a pretense to failing. And this is the very same reason why you should set your sails for your journey. You never know if you will fail or succeed. A ship that never sails out of the port will never discover the sea. And a good captain of a ship who sets his sails on a journey knows that the wind does not always blow in his favor. In fact, the wind may even set him back. The knowledge that the wind may set him back does not deter him from going on the journey. He instead learns to navigate through rough waters and unfavorable winds. Why does he continue with such persistence? Because he knows that though the journey is long and that he might not even reach his destination, he is already experienced more life than someone who did not. It is in knowing how to overcome your limitations, through wisdom and knowledge, is the key to becoming successful. Everyone fails at some time or another, but those who learn from their experiences tend to succeed later in life, but in greater fashion. Every single day, I have to remind myself to seek out new experiences and try new things. Even the smallest of life experiences can change us. And changing our lives for the better requires new experiences.

Only you measure success. You set your own thresholds, standards, and definitions of succeeding and failing. Once you determine your goals, you need to determine how much time you will spend working towards them. It is a long and hard road to success, but you must also determine if you are willing to spend time and energy and whether your goals are worth the pain or not. There is no such thing as instant or easy success. Anyone who ever set forth on a successful journey knows that every drop of sweat and every sleepless night, were necessary to achieve their dreams. Even good riders fall and great archers miss, but they never cease doing what they love to do. Remember that failing only begins when you begin to end your journey.

Our very existence in life is a journey in itself, comprised of many decisions. The differences between one story and another are the decisions made along the way. The World is filled of wonders and beauty; whether we choose to be a part of it makes all the difference. The experiences we have and how we react to them, define who we are. My point here is that venturing forth on something new can open a whole new world of experiences. Do not let fears of failure or uncertainty limit your experiences in life.

"Who has no faults? To err and yet be able to correct it is best of all." --Yaun-Wu

CHAPTER THREE

The Beginner's Mind

"Every child is born a genius."
--Albert Einstein

The room was musty and the stench of sweat permeated from the floor. We were all kneeling with our eyes closed, formed into a perfect circle. I was concentrating on my breathing while my heart was pounding deeply in my chest. My sensei called me into the center of the circle. I knew what was about to happen. He was going to test my martial skills. At the time, I was only sixteen years old but my sensei was closer to sixty. I jumped to my feet and entered the circle where I was to spar with him. Sensei personified the traditional martial artist. He was not big in stature nor was he muscular. It was quite the opposite. He barely weighed in at 110 pounds. He wore this old tattered Gi (martial arts uniform) and his black belt was so faded it almost white in color. By all natural rights, I had the advantages; youth, speed, and strength. He beckoned for me to advance and attack. I was already planning what fancy move I was going to do in order to take him down. In that same second I executed three roundhouse kicks and then a spinning back kick, followed up with two front punches. This was a very fancy and complicated combination that would take down most opponents on the street. Before I could even complete my second roundhouse kick, I found myself on that putrid floor, looking up at the dimly light ceiling. Sensei extended his hand down so he could help me up. I shamefully stumbled back into place in the circle. He then told me he beat me because he had a 'white belt'. At the time I did not understand that statement, because he wasn't a white belt he was a grandmaster black belt....

Being a student of the martial arts has taught me my knowledge is only limited to my experiences. The sad contradiction is that the more knowledge we have, the more difficult to see beyond them. We slowly become bound and limited with more knowledge. In this, we must always keep an open mind and empty ourselves to the world. Shunryu Suzuki, a Zen Master, once said, "In the beginner's mind there are many possibilities, in the expert's there are few." He continued on to say that there are no enlightened people, but only enlightened activity. We should never confuse the difference of what we actually know to what we think we know. Once you can determine the difference, only then can you make room for inner growth. We can apply this philosophy to any aspect of our lives. According to Carl Jung, a German psychologist, children are born with an empty cognizance, which will be filled through life experiences. Very young toddlers, especially babies, have the innate ability to acquire knowledge at an amazing rate. They are like sponges that soak up the cup of knowledge. This ability can be attributed to their lack of knowledge. They have no prejudices or preconceptions about the world. Babies instinctively "know" that they know nothing. This only proves that in thinking that we know, we fail to comprehend the absolute truths. Knowledge is important but it is the imagination that holds the key to possibilities.

Approaching life with a beginner's mind offers us a potent ability to maintain an open mind. This open mindedness is an essential key to learning the secrets of the universe. Very young children tend to perceive the world with awe, thus making everything they see, hear, feel, and taste seem profoundly wonderful. If we can achieve this same level of open mindedness as adults, then we open the doorway to a higher level of learning and more importantly a higher level of experiencing the world. As adults, we already have biases that taints and sway our minds from the pureness of an experience. Past experiences are a very important part of who we are, but they should never be sole precedence of future ones. Being able to take each experience independently will lead you a purer experience that leads to a richer life. Some of the things that can limit the pureness of an experience are prejudices, fears, immorality, or greed. What we think we know today, may be proved to be wrong tomorrow. Being formless in all we do and know, will give us the greatest state of mind to learn and grow.

Looking back, now I understand what sensei meant by being a 'white belt.' Even though he had a black belt, his belt faded to white; and that white belt showed that even through mastery, there is always more to learn!

"You see things and say 'why?' but I dream things that never were and ask, 'why not?"
--George Bernard Shaw

CHAPTER FOUR

Knowledge and Wisdom

"I am defeated and know it if I meet any human being from which I find myself unable to learn anything."
-- George Herbert Palmer

I have been very fortunate in life, and especially had the opportunity to have lived abroad in Europe. During that time, I despised the military life imposed upon our family. We were constantly moving every couple years; from country to country; from base to base. Only after I graduated from college, did I really realize the richness that I experienced in so many different cultures. Few people share the luxury that I had growing up that came with constantly moving around the globe. With each new move we did, I kept learning from the cultures that surrounded me. For the same very reasons today, I am always trying to learn or do something new. People are always telling me that I am always in constant motion and starting new endeavors; but what they fail to understand is, I do things to simply learn more about it. So in my own interests, I slowly gain more knowledge to enrich my life. Keeping an open mind is critical in learning from new experiences. There is always something beautiful to learn even in the most mundane tasks. Remember, you are on your own personal journey, so each step you take can either be meaningful or wasted. We do not have to limit our experiences and knowledge by circumstance alone, but instead we can choose to seek it outwardly.

With the advent of the internet and the information age, knowledge sharing has become a common paradigm. But no matter how great the multimedia internet can be, nothing can compare to the tactility of a hard bound book or manuscript. Words written on paper are like incantations etched on scrolls of wisdom. Books allow you to use your own interpretations and perceptions about what the author is attempting to relay. Yet, the most powerful sources of knowledge are within our reach every day. Those sources are the people around you. Their experiences are far more eloquent and colorful than just words on a page. They can provide emotion and a narrative to their experiences. The mere expressions of the storyteller mold the tale they weave that sparks your own imaginations and perceptions. I once met a U.S Army Veteran named Joe who was at the Invasion of Normandy. (Yes, I know this sounds like a fabricated story from a bad book, but his name was actually Joe, as in G.I Joe.) You could feel the intense emotions in his voice and the somber sincerity in his eyes, as he shared with me his personal account of that dreadful day. My point is, that knowledge is all around us, just waiting to be shared. It is in a form of a book, an experience, or even a story of another. But the best kind of knowledge is one that is passed down from our elders, friends, and family. An essential part of listening to anyone's story, is to never belittle their experiences, for no matter how miniscule the tale is, they always hold an ounce of wisdom. More importantly it is not the amount of knowledge you have, it is how you use it. Listen to others, and learn from their mistakes. Take advices when you can and use them to your advantage. In return, you should pay forward by sharing your knowledge and experiences with others. People are more inclined to trade and share information when the information you provide is useful. Experiences often come in the form of advice. Using the advices that are imparted upon us is the like opening a book to questions we never had, yet we find later in life that those same advices hold inherent truth. Unfortunately, we cannot gain wisdom from other people's experiences; only knowledge that can prepare us for the future. Though the past is a great teacher, it will never replace what is in the immediate. Though experiences hold clues to the past, they are also limited by the memories of those dispensing them. Since these limitations occur on a human level, the advice you might receive may be somewhat misleading. The more knowledge you can collect from multiple sources, the better.

Lastly, having knowledge is only half of the equation – the other half is wisdom. Knowledge is learned and where wisdom is realized. Wisdom is a profound understanding and realizing of people, things, events or situations. Wisdom provides you with the ability to choose or act to consistently produce the ideal results with a minimum of time and energy. Wisdom is the ability to optimally (effectively and efficiently) apply perceptions and knowledge and so produce the desired results. Wisdom is comprehension of what is true or right coupled with optimum judgment as to action. It is believed that wise people sense, work with, and align themselves and others to life. In this view, wise people help others appreciate the fundamental interconnectedness of life. Simply put, having knowledge is not enough – we must have wisdom to apply that knowledge at the right time and place – principally when morality, ethics, and beliefs are implicated.

You might be wondering how the experiences and wisdom of others can help you in your own personal journey. Think of it as your own private library that you can access to help you prepare for the future. During your journey, you will come across many crossroads where uncertainty will loom over you. The knowledge and wisdom imparted onto you can be a guide when the path is obscure. Despite how much we prepare ourselves for the future, or how much wisdom and knowledge we have, there are no guarantees in life. We can never truly control an outcome; we can only influence it. Hopefully though, through knowledge and wisdom, that we gain insights to ourselves – which is the most important lesson we can learn.

"We can be knowledgeable with another man's knowledge, but we cannot be wise with another man's wisdom."
--Michel De Montaigne

A Journey of Insights

CHAPTER FIVE

Seasons Change

"Change your thoughts and you change your world."
--Norman Vincent Peale

During college I lived in my parents' house while they were stationed in Hawaii. Back then, the town was considered a fairly small farming community by California standards. I graduated from Cal-Davis in 1996 and moved away that same fall. It was not until the Christmas of 2003, when I came back to visit them. On our drive from the airport, I could not recognize the town or the streets. The once farm lands were now rows of condominiums and tract homes. The changes were significant, and even as we approached my parent's house, it no longer seemed familiar. I felt a bit somber by such the changes but yet comforted to the fact that I too had grown beyond this reminiscent past. Nothing in life holds permanent certainty and thus with every passing breath I take, is different from the one before. In life, change is both the anticipated, and tragically inevitable. "Change has a considerable psychological impact on the human mind. To the fearful it is threatening because it means that things may get worse. To the hopeful it is encouraging because things may get better. To the confident it is inspiring because the challenge exists to make things better." (King Whitney Jr.)

No matter how much we hold on to the present and the way things are; they will always change. As humans, we are creatures of habit and comfort, but unfortunately, the world is in a state of continuous movement. Even the smallest molecules and atoms are in constant motion and flux. Without change, life would be stagnant and predictable. Many times in our journey and individual lives, we will face change. Sometimes those changes are welcome, while other times they bring us heartache. In our journeys, we must understand that the road we mapped out may not be the one we end up travelling. What we must learn to do is to embrace change as it comes. We must become part of the change or be left behind ourselves. Be like the ocean; ever changing, ever moving, and ever beautiful. It is always important to remember that all endeavors begin with change. And every action is a state of change in itself.

There will be many events of change that can derail us from our life journey. We must learn to accept that change, may cause distress, and can also leave you to be disheartened; however, remember these feelings will pass as well. Since we cannot envision future outcomes, it is difficult to see beyond the pain. In some cases, the pain today caused by unexpected change, may actually be a blessing tomorrow. This is particularly true when our own hearts are on the line. The lover's breakup causes heartache for many, it feels like the end of the world. However, the breakup comes as a welcome hindsight when true love emerges later in life. Some things are meant to happen in order to accommodate and make room for the newer and better things in life. There are many changes in life that can happen in a blink of an eye that can catch us off balance.

On the other hand, change can happen in a gradual and slow process. There will be times when you will yearn for the winds of change to blow swiftly to set transition in action. Sometimes the change is so slow that it is unnoticeable. And when the change occurs, it is as much a surprise as an abrupt change. When change is slow it is natural, transformative, and seemingly uninfluenced. The truth is all change is a result of the millions of ripples in the universe caused by individual stones, just as I mentioned in chapter one. Just like time itself, the wheels of fate are constantly turning, changing everything. The natural universe is on its own clock, responsible for the chaos and reordering of all life.

Whether you experience gradual change or rapid change, change is both inevitable and required. Change will keep your life challenging, interesting, and most of all, worth living. The change that brings turmoil and hardship is never welcome, but is just as necessary as the ones that brings bliss and elation. A cup which is never emptied can never be refilled with the newer water. Thusly so, change will bring good things into your life. Throughout all the changes in my life, I have learned this lesson: Changes of hardship taught me how to weep and be strong; Changes of joy taught me how to laugh and be grateful; but in both cases, change taught me how to live.

"Nothing endures but change."
--Heraclitus

CHAPTER SIX

The Rain Must Fall

"Life can be understood backwards; but it must be lived forwards."
--Soren Kierkegaard

At the time, I was a very young Lieutenant in the US Army, and was going about my daily duties. It was a beautiful spring day in May, as I admired the blueness in the sky and the warmth touch my face, as I noticed one of my female soldier walking with distraught towards the barracks. I caught up to her and asked her what was bothering her. With tears in her eyes and trembling voice, she turned and told me that she just lost her unborn baby. My heart suddenly saddened and I couldn't do anything to help her. I later told her everything happens for a reason and she had to be strong. Even though I made her feel somewhat better, I know that she suffered a terrible and heartbreaking lost.

We all suffered under the hands of lost at one point or another. Whatever that lost is, we always feel like the world was crumbling down on us. Lost is a very difficult event to deal with in life, unfortunately, it is an event that we must accept and face in all of our lives. Becoming angry and depressed is a natural human reaction to such an experience, but those two emotions are almost as effective as trying to raise the dead. It is absolutely acceptable to feel sad and empty. You know what I am referring to, if you ever lost a loved one to death. There are no tricks or secrets on how to deal with the tribulations of this kind of loss. I can only say that things do happen for a reason. Life has a strange but effective way of balancing everything out. For every loss there is one gain in the continuum. We may not find solace in this but we choose to live life with conviction and passion. We must find strength where there is weakness.

When you were born, you did not know what was beyond birth, so you did not fear birth. So how come, you fear death when you don't what is beyond it. Death is considered the ultimate loss that anyone can experience. But our limited perception of death restricts our ability to understand its part in universe. Death brings value in our lives, and makes us appreciate the time we have in this world. The day you were born is the day you started to die. We may not like it but just like life, death is all around us. In death, we must remember that nothing is permanently lost; instead it is a metamorphosis into another world. Even in the agony of loss, we must remember to sustain hope; as it is in hope that fuels our dreams of a better tomorrow.

There will be many other types of tribulations that you will encounter in life. Some will be easy to overcome, while others will take years to surmount. Life will be filled with many struggles to triumph over. Dread, hopelessness, loss, death, injustice, and numerous more soul breaking events may haunt us as we journey down the road of life. We all have to fight these battles within ourselves. Love ones and friends may give you strength to persevere, but you alone must defeat these elements of hopelessness. True, loss is inevitable, but so is gain. Do not concentrate on what you have lost, but be grateful for what you have today, and what the future may provide. Remember that the universe is in constant state of mutability to maintain a balance. Where there is loss, there will be gain. Where there is death, there will be life. Where there is emptiness, it will be filled again in time. Nature must take away the old to make room for the new; that is the circle of life. The sun cannot shine all the time - the rain must fall in order for life to continue to grow. Know that life will test your limits. Whether you endure and preserve your resolve; or let your convictions be eroded, is up to you. In either case, remember, that these are the moments will define you.

"The world is so constructed, that if you wish to enjoy its pleasures, you also must endure its pains."
--Swami Brahmananda

CHAPTER SEVEN

Living in The Now

"We take a handful of sand from the endless landscape of awareness around us and call that handful of sand the world."
--Robert M. Pirsig

I have questioned my existence in life so many times, that I have ran out of questions to ask myself. Questions like 'where am I going', 'who am I', and 'what am I doing' have come to thought over and over again. I am sure you have done this as well. These questions become even more prevalent during times of personal adversity. Since I myself have been searching for my own resolutions, I cannot provide you with answers for your own life. The words in this book will have different meanings for each person, and moreover it will even evolve for each person over time. Every individual has their own perceptions of reality, but despite the innumerable point of views, there is only one true reality. Even though there are unlimited sights, unlimited sounds, and unlimited feelings, there is only one existing veracity. A fault in human cognizance is that we function and focus on limited perception rather than perceiving the totality of the experience, thus we distort and impair the holistic experience. Furthermore, as our lives become busier, we have the propensity to focus on outcomes rather than existing in the present. By doing so, we can miss meaningful details and diminish the overall quality of the experience. Awareness of the moment is more important than the end. However, do not confuse the end with the final results. The end implies completion, while results defines quality. In a fast paced world of automation and instantaneous gratification, we tend to overlook these simple details that make up the totality of the experience. It is in these details that enhance and define the axiom of our life experiences. What do I mean by that? For instance, when was the last time you really watched a sunrise instead of diving straight into your emails? When was the last time you simply really listened to the pattering of the rain, instead of complaining about the bad weather? Or when was the last time you simply felt the sand in your toes, instead about worrying about work during your vacation? It seems that we are always caught up in trying to be somewhere, finishing a work project, or just dredging our way towards the weekend. As a result of always trying to pursue the end and not appreciating or living in the moment; we miss out on the small miracles in life. Inadvertently, we subconsciously isolate ourselves from the unfolding world. This isolation is like standing on one side of a glass window; and the side you are on is empty; while the other side is life and all of its glorious mysteries. However, the mysteries of life are not mysteries at all. They are merely the reflections of what you consciously chose to ignore in this world. Most people fail to appreciate the world in its fullest, because they are too concerned with only themselves.

Living in the now, requires us to completely and consciously acknowledge our environment. Heaven and earth are an integral part of the world we live in. The sky above us and the ground beneath us surround our essences daily. We are bound by nature, no matter how much we hide from it. When it rains, do you not seek shelter? When it is sunny, do you not go out? When it is cold, do you not seek heat? And when it is hot, do you not seek shade? Whether we like it or not, our actions are directly influenced by the universe. We must appreciate everything that exists, because therein lies the magic, the miracles, and the mysteries. The key to unlocking these mysteries is to be fully aware of them as they occur. One must experience life as it is, naturally and untainted. We must look at the world void of biases or preconceptions. Opinions are essential to arouse thought and provoke examination, but opinions can distort reality. We must appreciate everything within our sights, both the beautiful and the horrid – as it is just personal opinions anyway. Only when we learn to do this and free ourselves from personal partialities, can we really become one with existence. With clear thought we can understand the perfection of balance that existed since time itself; chaos and harmony, good and evil, motion and stillness, change and constancy.

When we pay attention to the details through perceiving and embrace the actual moment, we get a better understanding and appreciation for those moments, thus learning more about that moment and ourselves. In action, we gain knowledge, and in knowledge we gain awareness. In action, do not be too concerned about deviations from the original intent, as sometimes taking a different approach may bring you closer to it. Taking a different path can precede you to new ideas. The bottom line, is to focus on the task at hand, but never forget your goal. When you are aware of perceiving, you are engulfing yourself in life as it transpires. We tend to look and believe only in the visible, but even then we look with discriminate eyes. To live for each and every moment of your life is the hardest thing, but when you achieve this state, then you will learn to live life as it was meant to be. Too often do we desire to finish the race and not enjoy the run. Though as difficult as it may be at times, we must strive to enjoy what is presented before us.

As I write this chapter and rush to complete it, I find myself not owning this experience. And I too am guilty for doing exactly what the unknown author is saying in the following:

"First I was dying to finish high school and start college. And then I was dying to finish college and start working. And then I was dying to marry and have children. And then I was dying for my children to grow old enough so I could return to work. And then I was dying to retire. And NOW, I am dying and suddenly realize I forgot to live."

The magic and wonders of life is all around us if we take time to really *experience* them. The journey we take is far more beautiful and intricate if we take the time to fully appreciate the scenery. The mysteries encompassing about you will not all be solved, because they were never meant to be solved. However, you will have a far better understanding of reality; that there is a universal connection. You will understand that all actions result from other actions. For everything you do in life, put your heart into it, and enjoy, for it may be your only chance to.

"We look backward too much and we look forward too much; thus we miss the only eternity of which we can be absolutely sure --the eternal present, for it is always now."
--William Phelps

CHAPTER EIGHT

In Pursuit of Dreams

"No one knows what he can do until he tries."
--Syrus

Being a product of the 80's music scene where hair bands, heavy metal, and MTV ruled, I was like any other teenager of that time; I wanted to play electric guitar. However, my father was a Sergeant in the US Army and came from a strict Catholic upbringing, and he did not approve. I begged him for a guitar but with to no avail did I get one. My only option was to earn it myself. That year, I took a summer job on the Army base that paid $3.25 an hour, which was minimum wage back then. I eventually saved enough money to buy my best friends guitar that sat idle in his closet. For the rest of the year I taught myself how to play guitar using tablature, chord books, and by ear. Of course back then the internet or YouTube did not exist so I was completely on my own. For the next 2 years, I practiced until I sounded decent. My dream was to become a lead guitarist in a rock band. During college, I played in several bands, and a few gigs. For four years of college I did this, but eventually I ended up joining the military myself. Obviously, that dream of becoming a famous rock god never came to reality. You know what did come true though, my dream of being a guitarist. I may not the fame or fortune but nonetheless I have accomplished how to play guitar.

In the pursuit of any dream, many times we lose sight of what really shapes and molds our lives. And many times the dream we think we want, is not the dream we need in life. The important thing to note is that regardless of the unforeseen outcome, you must choose to simply 'just do'. Don't worry about being good at it, or pleasing others, the skill and talent will eventually come with persistence and dedication. If you always wanted to paint, then paint. If you want to sing, then sing. Being good at it or having the immediate talent should not prevent you from doing what you want to do. Even the most talented people needed their skills to be honed and forged. No one is exempt from putting in the time and hard work in achieving their goals. The more you invest into anything, the more it invests back to you – it is only a matter of time. When Pablo Picasso first started painting, the majority thought that his portraits were horrific and unsightly, but today those same paintings are deemed priceless. As everything else in the world, talent is really relative. The things that are considered to be of no value today may be considered as a piece of artwork tomorrow; and you will always have tomorrow. As you begin your journey, be mindful to be adaptable to the unknown and unfamiliar. This will enable you to unhindered and unconstrained to acquire new knowledge, thus gradually and constantly improving yourself. Adaptability will also provide you with the tolerance to deal with downfalls and the constitution to persevere.

The heart of achievement begins in action. Achievement does not occur instantaneously; instead it is a laborious task. Starting what is necessary in order to initiate action is a great attribute of the doers. Doing what is essential in order to maintain perpetuate action that leads to success is the attribute of the great. The world will challenge you to many resistances that will cause you to feel inept. Stress and friction will cause you to fail at times. The truth is that anything worth achieving is worth fighting for. A bird's feathers are made to catch air, thus creating air resistance. At first glance, the air resistance may seem to be unfavorable, but the closer you examine the larger scheme of nature, that same air resistance is what make birds fly. Without the air resistance, the feather would not catch air, and thus the bird is grounded. All I am saying is that sometimes resistance is necessary in order to make something worthwhile. The achievement that requires no effort is no achievement at all.

People fail "to do", due to a variety of reasons, but these are not reasons at all, but rather excuses. Nothing in this world is perverse or troublesome that it cannot be overcome with heart, soul, and mind. On the contrary, people succeed more when difficult tasks are set out before them. The instrument of talent is seeing beauty in the smallest of details and being able to adapt to changes. It is the small insignificant tasks that we tend to blow off and not bother with. So with that piece of advice, stop posting about others peoples achievements and start making your own and living a life worth remembering.

"Only those who will risk going too far can possibly find out how far one can go."
--T. S. Eliot

CHAPTER NINE

The Thief of Dreams

"Strength doesn't come from physical capacity. It comes from indomitable will."
--Mahatma Gandhi

Without courage or determination, achievement becomes virtually impossible, since these are elements to success. To accomplish any task whether big or small, it is essential to find these qualities within ourselves. Too often fear and uncertainty can hinder even the most motivated person from succeeding or venturing forth into the unknown. Ultimately, it is fear that blinds us from truly experiencing the beauty that surrounds us. It is fear that prevents almost all human actions. We are all susceptible to fear and have experience its debilitating effect in some manner. We cannot remove fear nor completely will it away. We can only accept it and understand its nature. It is in this understanding that we can start to overcome this ignorant dread. Fundamentally, fear is nothing more than an unfavorable but imagined outcome. In other words, we think the worse outcome is going to occur. The essential problem is that this can paralyze you from actually achieving. The simplest analogy I can use to demonstrate this is the fear of asking someone out on a date. Have you ever been afraid to ask another person for a date? In my adolescent years, I was so terrible and fearful of this. However, as I matured, I began to understand one thing; that despite I was rejected or not, it actually made me less fearful on the next attempt. In actuality, today I became very good approaching people in general as I learned from those experiences. Two famous quotes come to mind when dealing with fear:

"Courage is not the absence of fear,
but rather the judgement that something else
is more important than fear." --Ambrose Redmoon

"A great part of courage is the courage of having done
the thing before."--Ralph Waldo Emerson

These two quotes sums of the fabric of courage. The act of repeating an action and finding something more important than fear (and in most cases), more important than you; will give you the ability to overcome this malingering enemy. As you begin to overcome fear, the stronger your willpower becomes; and more likely you are to succeed. It is positive perpetual effect.

As you gain courage, it is easy to also become lost in it. Success not only breeds achievement but also arrogance. Arrogance then breeds foolish actions. The fine line between foolishness and courage is difficult to discern; and this is where wisdom becomes important. But how do we know the difference if we lack that wisdom? The answer is simple. Foolishness is reckless and does not consider consequences to others. Foolish actions are those that are born of pride, envy, mal-intentions and derived solely on personal gain. Courageous actions are born of kindness, values, humility, and selflessness. We, as humans, are not infallible, and we will mistakenly identify foolishness for courage. Unfortunately, when this happen, someone else always get hurt in the process. That is the ultimate discernment between courageous acts and foolish acts. The question must be asked "Who can get hurt?" The message here is to simply be mindful and weary that too much courage can lead to a darker path.

In conclusion, I am not saying fear is all bad. In fact, being fearless is nothing more than controlled fear. The secret is not to let fear control you but you control it. In the end we do not want fear to be dictating how we live our lives or prevent us from truly experiencing life. It will always be fear that will keep you from stepping through any door in life. If there is one thing you should remember from this chapter, it is that "Fear is the thief of all dreams".

"There are costs and risks to a program of action, but they are far less than the long range risks and costs of comfortable inaction."
--John F. Kennedy

CHAPTER TEN

Paths of Destiny

"Life is a journey. When we stop, things don't go right."
--Pope Francis

I stood there a fork in the road as ominous as it could be; I could either continue down this path or choose to make a prodigious turn. Both ways would be filled with pain and heartache, but the choice nonetheless remained in front of me. Life had finally brought me to this inevitable choice. I knew no matter the decision, I would always think to myself, "Did I make the right choice." I had questions looking in front of me and I have questions looking behind me. My mother is a very religious person, and she always said to me, "God has a plan for everyone." If this is true, then that means we are powerless in our own lives. To an extent it may seem that way, but nothing is further from the truth. I am believer that we are in control of our choices and that we _do_ have a destiny. However, the potential to achieve that destiny is comprised of our choices in life. This may sound like a contradiction, but let me explain.

Think of life as a road map filled with many splitting roads between two points; one being an origination and the other a destination. The paths between those two points can be travelled in many ways. You can take the most direct straight line path, or take the winding turns of detours, turns, side roads, back roads, and other divergences. The choices you make puts you on different roads and each road differs. Some roads are made of gravel and rougher, yet some roads are paved highways and smoother. Some roads have a better scenery yet others are drab. Each road, have different pit stops and different people along the way. No matter which way you take, and no matter how long you take to get there, the destination is always the same. The choices you make in your journey can make the ride there a pleasant one or a rough one. The important thing to remember is enjoy the moments and understand that some choices will make it a difficult journey sometimes. Sometimes we will make bad decisions that will discourage us and prevent us from looking ahead. Making a bad decision does not necessarily mean you made the wrong one. This is not the time to feel depressed and halfhearted – instead this is the time to move forward and make the best with what you have. It is human nature to feel self-pity and sorrow, but remember this is just page in your journey of life. Better things are ahead of you if you allow life into your heart.

Destiny is a funny concept. It implies that we have preordained place in life, and too often we may think we can never achieve our individual destinies. There are two reasons why we may think this way. It is possible to never achieve your potential destiny. The first reason is that along the journey we consciously chose a different destination. As individuals, we each choose what we think is right for us in our lives. I once dreamed of being rock star, and obviously that did not happen. I made a conscious decision to pursue other things in life, and I ultimately changed my destination. Why did I do this? Maybe it was easier, or maybe it was the right decision at the time, or maybe it was the demise of my dream. Whatever the outcome, I cannot regret my decisions since I made them. I simply changed my destination – hence no regrets. The second reason is we simply never reach any destination of our choosing. Life is like a vehicle. Imagine a car traveling across the nation. It can only go so far as it has gasoline or even before it breaks down. Like that car, we only have so much time and energy to get where we want to go. We can actually end somewhere where we never intended to be in the first place. Now, this does not mean it is a terrible fate. It just means we spent so much on the journey we forgot the destination. I previously mentioned to live in the now and experience life; however, there is always a fine balance between experiencing the now but always seeking the destination. Both can be achieved with a little thought and wisdom.

In both cases, notice that conscious decisions can and will affect your overall destiny. In both cases, the results may be undesirable, but nonetheless, it does not mean you made the wrong decisions in life. As you learn from each decision and travel down your path, you will gain valuable lessons. With age, comes experience, with experience comes wisdom, and with wisdom comes the ability to fully comprehend situations that require decision making. In the end, the power of choice lays within your hands.

"Fate's eventuality is cruel, in that it does gives you what you want; but usually at the wrong right time."
--Elm Valle

CHAPTER ELEVEN

Lessons Not Regrets

"Looking back, of course, it was irresponsible, mad, forlorn, idiotic, but if you don't take chances then you'll never have a winning hand, and I've no regrets."
--Bernard Cornwell

In 1994, I was given an opportunity to accept a full grant to attend Stanford University in California. Being young and foolish, I turned it down so I could pursue other interests. Instead, I went to Solano Community College and afterwards to University of California, Davis. While at Davis, I completed the ROTC program and earned my commission as a Second Lieutenant in the US Army. Many people would say that was a mistake, given the fact that Stanford is a highly acclaimed university. Sometimes, I do wonder what my life would be like if I had chosen that path. Would my life be better now or would I be more successful today? I will never know, but there is one thing I do know – it is that I do not regret that decision. Someone once said

"No regrets, just lessons. No worries, just acceptance. No expectations, just gratitude. Life is too short." It really took a while for me to really understand that statement. In my younger years, I was filled with anger and regret and I blamed the world for my own actions. Now, I have come to realization that my every decision was a lesson on how navigate through adversity. My military experience has been invaluable to me and has given me tools and experiences in life that most people can only imagine. Those same experiences shaped my beliefs and given me strength throughout the years. Those seemingly so called 'mistakes' forged me into who I am today. Regardless of the enormity of the mistake, each mishap provides each one of us with an opportunity to learn a valuable lesson.

Rules for Being Human

1. *You will learn lessons.*
2. *There are no mistakes—only lessons.*
3. *A lesson is repeated until it is learned.*
4. *If you don't learn easy lessons, they get harder.*
   (Pain is one way the universe gets your attention.)
5. *You'll know you've learned a lesson when your actions change.*

--Author Unknown

In the previous chapter, I talked about how life is a road map filled with turns and decisions. Too often in life, we fail to see the value of the 'road less taken.' What is worse, we regret decisions made. You may feel regretful for something you *did do*, but I guarantee you, that you feel more regret on the things you *did not do*. Obviously, this does not mean that there no mistakes in life. As humans we are all bound to make mistakes. It is important that we learn from those mistakes – and in those lessons, can we truly live life without regrets.

Living life without regret, does not mean living it completely reckless however. Making reckless decisions without thought is the fool's philosophy. Decisions are always meant to be thought through and weighed. Sometimes there is a 'better' choice – notice I did not say a 'right' choice. The 'better' choice enhances our lives in a positive manner; while the 'worse' choice will provide us lessons through pain. That is the key difference. A reckless decision is simply not weighing the options set before you. Living a life without regret means you understand the lessons of each 'mistake' and the purpose of each decision.

So what does it truly mean to live a life without regrets? It simply means that you will make mistakes; You will take the 'worse' of paths sometimes; And that you will feel pain and heartache often; But in the end, the sum of those experiences will give you a life worth remembering. It will make you who you are; and with every experience, good or bad, it will become the fabric of your soul. Living a life without regret is appreciating life to the fullest: all the joys, the sorrows, the warmth, the bitter cold, the tears of laughter and the tears of pain. I had my fair share of tribulations and when I feel like the world is about to collapse on me I always remember this: "God grant me the serenity to accept the things I cannot change, the courage to change the things I can, and the wisdom to know the difference." (Reinhold Niebuhr). Through my experiences, my view of the world began to change, and it led me to believe that there are no coincidences in life. I believe that every decision set before you, is there to provide opportunities; and that every person we meet in our journey was placed there for a reason. With each decision comes a lesson that you were meant to learn to serve you in the future. And each person you come across will shape your world. Often we will not understand at the time because we are too occupied with dealing with the emotions that come with those events. But just know that everything passes and only the lessons will remain. You will have to choose between ignoring or learning from those lessons. Whatever you choose though remember to simply be grateful for them; for without them means there is no growth in your soul. Lastly, remember that life is short and that 'We live in deeds, not years; in thoughts, not breaths;' (Philip James Bailey).

"Accept everything about yourself - I mean everything. You are you and that is the beginning and the end - no apologies, no regrets."
--Henry A. Kissinger

A Journey of Insights

CHAPTER TWELVE

The Magic Within

"Snowflakes are one of nature's most fragile things, but just look what they can do when they stick together."
--Vista M. Kelly

Truly living a life without regret is indeed a difficult task for anyone. Often times we are blinded by our own pains and sorrows, and we fail to see the beauty around and within us. The fact is, that we simply have to pause long enough to really see it. One of my most marvelous memories of living in Germany was the time I was at a winter retreat with my best friend in Berchtesgaden. Berchtesgaden is situated in the Bavarian Alps, near the border of Austria. It is known more for being Adolph Hitler's famous home called the Eagle's Nest. It is somewhat ironic that such beauty existed for such a mad man; but even a mad man knew the importance of beauty in life. A few miles south of Berchtesgaden lies Germany's most beautiful and cleanest Alpine Lake: Lake Konigssee. I was staying at a lodge close by to the Eagle's Nest. My best friend Manuel and I spent an entire week hiking, climbing, and exploring the mountainous terrain; taking in nature with every breath. On the last night, our group had climbed to the highest point of the mountain just right above Lake Konigssee. As we climbed, the only thoughts that ran through my head was to keep breathing as I was dizzy from the lack of oxygen due to the altitude. As we crested the top, I felt nothing but pain. My feet were numb from the freezing snow, my legs ached from the climb, and my lungs were burning through the cold air. As I slowly regained my composure, I looked up and realized that all that pain was worth it. It was the only time in my life, that I saw heaven and earth touch in one singular moment. Looking down into the lake, you can see the untouched virgin snow, the lake was serene like a mirror. The reflections of every mountain etched into the water. The sky was clear as could be, and every star seemed to be painted onto the night. The moon was fully illuminated and casted a soft glow over the landscape. No one in the group said a word; instead silence filled the cold night air. You could only hear the heavy breaths of each person. I could only but stare into this portrait. All at once I felt peace, serenity, awe, inspiration, and a sense of completeness. Within these brief moments, I felt what it meant to truly be surrounded by God's beauty. To this day, that memory is forever burned into my soul. The magic within is not something you see on the television of people doing disappearing acts or walking through walls. The magic within is the beauty of experience, and life itself. Pausing for the moment, and looking up beyond one's own pain, to witness what is in front of us.

In each of our lives, you must find that place where your heaven and earth meet. Find a place where the ocean's call can soothe your soul; Where the power of a whisper and the touch of a hand silences the world's discords. When the night arrives, let the stars guide you safely home. We all seek that heart-warming place to feel safe and complete. Life is full of magic and unbelievable wonders. The opening quote in this chapter about a snowflake is anecdote for life. Each snowflake is fragile and can be easily melted away with the slightest touch, yet when you have enough of them, they form a snowball. The snowball can be fashioned into anything your imagination desires. The snowflake represents the small joys in life: a walk in the park, hugs from your child, holding hand with a loved one, or even just watching the sun as it goes down. The world presents us with so much wonder and magic every day, but it is a shame that often times we miss them, or worse, take them for granted.

Furthermore, the magic we seek may not be far from ourselves. In fact, magic comes from within. Magic is simply the ability to see wonders with a child's heart. Magic is not trickery as stage magicians do, but knowing that life is the ultimate gift. Magic is the knowing that a possibility is limited only one's by courage and imagination. It is taking steps into a new journey and to awe at the discoveries.

We all have the power and strength to do anything we desire, and that is the magic that comes from within. Every child believes that his or her father is the strongest man alive. Why? Because the child believes that the father has superhuman strength. Since we were all children at one point, we still have the ability to see magic in our worlds, but we must bring forth that ability. As children we saw the world with such innocence and wonder. Everything we did was rooted in exploration and learning. Every first moment we experienced were magical; from the first time we learned about dinosaurs, to the first kiss, and to the first time you learned to ride a bike. Walt Disney understood the magic within us all, and he believed even as adults, we have the capacity to believe in that magic. He took our dreams and gave us back our childhood. He taught us a lesson that age is not a boundary, but simply a passageway. Age does not prevent us from believing in things. On the contrary, age should help us understand instead. However, with age most people become bitter and begin to separate from life's small wonders. We are caught up in everyday dilemmas and forget where we come from and where we need to go. That is the tragedy, we begin life with magic but as we age, we forget that magic. You can do anything you want, if your heart is in the right place. "These are magic years...and therefore magic days...and therefore magic moments (Anonymous)."

Life is not about getting somewhere but it is about the journey itself. Too many times we get where we want to go, but find ourselves not satisfied and once again longing to find something else. Life is simply living it the best you can with what you have and at the same time helping others along the way; this my friend is the magic which we all search for and need; love and acceptance.

"Enjoy yourself. These are the good old days you're going to miss in the years ahead."
--Unknown

A Journey of Insights

CHAPTER THIRTEEN

Matters of the Heart

"The greater the man's soul, the deeper he loves."
--Leonardo Da Vinci

We are all longing for that one single connection that ignites our hearts and makes us soar. Universally, Love can be magical in its very nature. It makes people do strange and wonderful things, and allows people to see beyond sight, and feel beyond prejudices. When it comes to matters of the heart, I must admit that I am not great at it. In my life, I have been hurt, and sometimes I am the one hurting someone else. The funny thing is, though we never truly want to hurt others, we often do. Humans do both wondrous and terrible things in the name of love. There are many great mysteries in the universe, let alone in the world - but the most mysterious and timeless element that transcends time and space is the word and feeling we call 'love'. Matters of the heart are definitely one of the most enigmatic and exciting aspects of life. The definition of love escapes us nor can we quite explain the way it can suddenly manifest itself into our lives. Poets, musicians, philosophers, and even scientist have all attempted to explain what love is. Is it a chemical reaction? Is it just a feeling in our soul? Does it come from the heart?

Love's elusive effects on people transcend any logical explanation. A person's heart tends to beat faster, as if they were struck with fear. Sweaty palms, dry lips, and a fluttering stomach resemble the symptoms of food poisoning. A person's mind is suddenly flushed with euphoria and glee. The world is suddenly a perfect place. Love is a very complex emotional experience that can place a person in a roller coaster ride. One moment love is an ideal emotion and the next, love becomes an object of hatred. Love is the proverbial double-edged sword, capable of healing and wounding. Love is a powerful word used throughout history. It is capable of bringing two people together or starting a war.

Since love stems from the heart, and not the mind, it will always seem illogical, unsound, and at times even immoral. Though we cannot fully explain what love is, we do know that it may come in many forms. I myself have experience three forms of love in my life: familial love, protective love, and romantic love. Sometimes I feel all three for a person, while others only one form. Actually C.S Lewis wrote a book in 1960 called (Lewis 1960). In his book he identifies four types of loves: Storge, Philia, Eros, and Agape.

Familial love (Storge) is simply the love you feel for a brother, sister, father, mother, or even a best friend. It is not associated with feeling of being "in love." Familial love is probably the easiest to identify with and simplest to define. Familial love is linked through the fondness of familiarity, family members or people who relate in familiar ways that have otherwise found themselves bonded by chance. It can be described as the most natural, emotive, and widely diffused of loves: natural in that it is present without coercion; emotive because it is the result of fondness due to familiarity; and most widely diffused because it pays the least attention to those characteristics deemed "valuable" or worthy of love and, as a result, is able to transcend most discriminating factors (C.S Lewis).

Protective (Philia) love happens with those you bonded with through friendships, common past experiences, or even past relationships. You feel compelled to protect and preserve the people whom you feel this protective love for. Protective love is about ensuring the well-being and welfare those whom you fell this type of love for.

The most talked about form of love is romantic love (Eros). Romantic love is subject of countless songs, poetry, and art. This is the most elusive form, because the feelings associated with romantic love is so abstract. A person will feel "in love" with another person. A complete sense of engulfed euphoria will overwhelm someone when feeling in love. When in love, you almost feel like you cannot live without that other person. You feel that the world is brighter and better when you are around him or her. Your very thoughts and actions are influenced by their mere presence. Their touch and scent becomes a longing that must be fulfilled. We all know how this kind of love feels, and we have an innate desire for this type of love. We seek it until our emotions are satisfied. It is an addiction within us all.

True love or unconditional love (Agape) is near impossible to find. It is a rare form of love that not easily changed or be broken. This kind of love makes the impossible, possible. True love is constant and forgiving in any situation. If and when you find true love, you will know it in your heart of hearts. In true love, forgiveness is not necessary, and it is completely unconditional. It serves and withstands regardless of changing circumstances.

Love is unpredictable and it materializes out of simplicity. Gestures of selflessness, kindness, and friendship nurtures simple bonds into love. Love is also devious in that it is formless and fluid – often changing. The love felt for another can change with time. Love's focus can jump from person to person – as humans easily fall in love. The intensity can increase or decrease. All of the changes are predicated by time and experience. A love un-nurtured is a love unattended; and a love unattended will soon fade. Tragically, too often, romantic love evolves, wanes, or even completely fade away. There are no guarantees in love. No one wants to inflict pain on another person, but that is part of the nature of love. Love's power transcends all boundaries. We cannot explain the mystery of love, because its very inscrutability is what defines it. In the course of your lifetime, you will face the adversity of love. You will be hurt and you will hurt someone; it is the natural course of love. So the question still remains: do each of us have a soul mate in which true love can be found? Only through time, patience, and faith, can that be answered. However, you look at love and what kind of love you feel, remember to never shut your doors to it - no matter the pain it may have caused you in the past - as it is love that inspires our capacity to reach further into life's beauty.

"To love at all is to be vulnerable. Love anything and your heart will be wrung and possibly broken. If you want to make sure of keeping it intact you must give it to no one, not even an animal. Wrap it carefully round with hobbies and little luxuries; avoid all entanglements. Lock it up safe in the casket or coffin of your selfishness. But in that casket, safe, dark, motionless, airless, it will change. It will not be broken; it will become unbreakable, impenetrable, irredeemable. To love is to be vulnerable."
--C.S. Lewis, The Four Loves

"It is impossible to love and be wise."
--Francis Bacon

"Love is the wisdom of the Fool, and the folly of the Wise."
--Samuel Johnson

"Love is something eternal; the aspect may change, but not the essence."
--Vincent Van Gogh

"When you have nothing left but love, then for the first time, you become aware that love is enough."
--Anonymous

"Love makes difficult things easy and almost unworthy of note."
--St. Thomas Aquinas

"Love gives naught but itself and takes naught from itself. Love possess not, nor would it be possessed; for love is sufficient unto love."
--Kahil Gibran
"Love is a canvass furnished by nature, and embroidered by imagination."
--Voltaire

"Love is a fiend, a fire, a heaven, a hell; where pleasure, pain, and sad repentance dwell."
--Richard Barnfield

CHAPTER FOURTEEN

Reflections of Passion

"One touch of nature makes the whole world kin."
--Shakespeare

I was sitting by my open window, looking out into the winter land. Everything resembled a portrait as the dark pastels blended the sky and the earth together making it difficult to determine where the sky started and the earth began. I can remember the sky was filled with a grayish color, and the smell of rain was ominous. The wind was whispering onto my face, in way that a mother touches a child's face. It had been so very long that I've seen my family. I missed my mother, my father, and my brothers. I had no one here; so far away from home, and I felt alone. My heart sank deeply into my chest, as I thought about the simple joys of home. Then suddenly, a raindrop kissed my cheek, then another, and another. The rain started to blanket the landscape in a shroud water. It wasn't raining hard, but instead it came in a slow, gentle, and rhythmic way. The rain played an echoing but soothing beat upon the roof. The wind picked up a little, from a breeze to a strong constant gust. The rain made me miss home that much more, as I reflected back to the old house. I used to watch the rain the same way from my old room as I watched it here now. The silence in the room resounded in my soul, as I realized that my face was not wet by the rain alone, but with my own tears. I don't remember much of the rest of that day, but I do remember looking out to the sky as I silently wept my heart out hoping that in some way the rain would bring my tears back home. I did not stop lamenting until the rain stopped and the sun began to break through the clouds with rays of light. That night I felt better though, as I went outside to greet the night and stars. The crisp night air embraced me into the vastness of the shimmering veil before me, and I felt invigorated and renewed. My sorrows earlier that day held a purpose. It seemed as if that whole ritual of crying did bring me to closer to heaven, but more importantly I felt a little closer to home.

Sometimes all we need is a good outflow of emotions to clear our souls. Emotions are keys to creativity and imagination. To be without emotion is to live life without passion. Expression is the greatest form of communication given to us. We can express ourselves through art, music, poetry, and dance, but most of the time we express our emotions through our own actions. There have been times in my life when I was simply overwhelmed by life's sorrows and I all I wanted to do was breakdown. In fact, that's exactly what I did. Those emotions were an expression of who I am. Our emotions are our way to express our love, appreciation, disapproval, content, fear, and much more. Unfortunately, the show of emotions in our society today may be seen as a sign of weakness. On the contrary, I believe it gives us strength when we least expect it. When you express your emotions then a part of you grows. More importantly, the person with whom you share your emotions grows as well. If we all take the time to share our emotions with one another, then we would have a better understanding of each other. A lot of pain and anxiety could be spared. Too often do we judge others by misconceptions and predeterminations. The reality, is that we all feel the need to express emotions in some form. Those who are unwilling to share themselves will be entrapped in their own self-made walls. By expressing our passions through music, poetry, or even writing, we each contribute to humanity something unique and heartfelt.

I guess what I am trying to say is that if we do not express ourselves, then we fail what is inherent to be human; to cry, to laugh, to sing, to write, to feel, to share, and to love. The very essence of humanity is the ability to have passions, and more importantly the ability to share them with others. After all, is it not the ability to connect with others that allows us to grow spiritually and cognitively?

The passion for life and the passion within our hearts is what drives and defines our existence as humans. Through these emotions can we convey the passions in our lives. Without them, we are simply empty shells. Without them, our actions become mechanical and meaningless. So much of our decisions are influenced by those same passions and emotions. It gives life to our actions and breath to our cause. Thus it is important to reflect on not only the decisions we make, but the fundamental reasons behind them. When we reflect on them, then only can we begin to understand ourselves. It also allows us to move forward in life. It gives us insight into what is important in our lives. It provides us with purpose in all we do. At the same time, we must also learn to let them go when the time is right. When we hold on too long to certain emotions, especially negative ones, it can hold us back from progressing into the next phase of our lives. As we grow through life, our passions will change. This is definitely apparent as we move through our teenage years and into adulthood. Different aspects of life become more important. If we held on to every childhood passion, we would definitely have a difficult time maturing. The lesson here is that be passionate in what you do. Pour your soul into what you love, and reflect on them. Learn who you are, and learn what life means to you. And always remember to let passion drive you but let reason guide you.

"Every great dream begins with a dreamer. Always remember, you have within you the strength, the patience, and the passion to reach for the stars to change the world."
--Harriet Tubman

CHAPTER FIFTEEN

The Seven Vices

*"Be at war with your vices, at peace with your neighbors, and
let every new year find you a better man."*
--Benjamin Franklin

Looking back on the past 20 years, I have done a
lot of wrong; not only to myself, but to others; and often
at times when success had given me wings. Just like
Icarus who flew too high to the sun, I too was a victim
of my own hubris. The unfortunate matter is that vices
are never realized in singular fashion, but manifest as a
collective. The worst part about vices is that they
manifest even in the best of intentions. Having passion
is like lighting a flame. It provides light, warmth, and
fuel; unattended that flame can become uncontrollable
and may consume everything in its path. When that
flame grows into a raging fire, your passions can turn
into a vice. There are seven main vices that are also

known as the seven deadly sins in the Bible: Lechery, Gluttony, Avarice, Hubris, Wrath, Envy, and Sloth. You do not have to be religious to know that these vices can be destructive. Unfortunately, these feelings are inherent to all human beings. They are emotions and passions that we all possess and are some of the strongest that you may feel. We must first understand each of these vices in order be able to recognize them and be mindful of our actions.

Lechery or Lust is the intense longing of desire for general immorality such as money, power, and unbridled sex. Wanting power, money or sex is not innately evil, as these are all necessary to survive. However solely seeking these things without considerations to consequences or seeking them for their own purposes is the catalyst for a path of evil intentions. At the heart of its folly, lust is not simply associated with sex, but the desire for concepts or objects that have no value to our spiritual bearing. The antipodal is Chastity.

Gluttony or overindulgence is the act of excessiveness to the point of unnecessary wastefulness. Too much of anything can be detrimental to both our bodies and soul. When we obtain too much of anything, we lose sight of its value, and we start to take them for granted. An object, concept, or even a person taken for granted becomes lost to us over time. The antipodal is Temperance (or Self Control).

Avarice or Greed is an artificial, rapacious desire and pursuit of material possessions. Avarice is usually the predecessor of Gluttony and the sister of Lechery. Avarice is more concentrated on materialism. The antipodal is Charity.

Hubris or Pride is the absence of humility and possessing the irrational belief that one is automatically and essentially better than others, failing to acknowledge the accomplishments of others, inflated self-importance, and excessive admiration of the personal self. The antipodal is Humility.

Wrath or Anger is a sense uncontrolled feelings of rage, and even hatred, often revealing itself in the wish to seek vengeance. Wrath, in its purest form, presents with injury, violence, and hate. The antipodal is Patience.

Envy or Covetousness can be described as a sad or resentful covetousness. Envy differs from Avarice where it focused towards the traits or possessions of someone else. In other words, you simply want what someone else has in a highly comparative measure. The antipodal is Kindness.

Sloth or Without Care can be characterize as having no emotional, physical, or spiritual care about oneself or others. It is more than just laziness, it is truly an absence of care to grow, learn, improve, or progress. The antipodal is Diligence.

Does this mean that we must eradicate all vices from our lives? Does that mean vices are the root of evil? The answer is no. Having absolutely no vices is not feasible. Living a life without vices, is to not live at all. We must first acknowledge that we all have vices. Then we need to understand each one, and learn to balance them in our lives. The goal is to understand them and balance them with virtues. Furthermore, we must to learn to respect and minimize their negative effects on others. Doing more good than harm onto others is the aspiration. However, that does not mean each good deed cancels out one bad deed. What I am trying to say is that, we need to take considerations of our own actions and how it can affect others. And by knowing that these vices have a destructive nature, then can we learn to not to easily fall prey to them. Even though vices are not seen as desirable human characteristics, they do have their place. They are as necessary as the air we breathe, and can also be the seed of our passions. "Passions are vices or virtues to their highest powers." (Johann Wolfgang von Goethe). Both Virtues and Vices, give us emotions and passions. Without one or the other, we become one dimensional and predictable. The best we can do is to be mindful of them and their consequences. And most importantly, control them so that they cannot not consume us or those we love.

"The passions of the young are vices in the old."
--Joseph Joubert

A Journey of Insights

CHAPTER SIXTEEN

The Seven Virtues

"Those who excel in virtue have the best right of all to rebel, but then they are of all men the least inclined to do so."
--Aristotle

With the proliferation of social media, it seems that humanity is starting to lose its virtues at an accelerated pace. The importance of self and individuality has become the focus of ideology for the generation born within this information age. The broadcasting of what is worn, eaten, traveled, or done permeates our society (known as 'posting' or 'posts' in social media). Furthermore, these same posts are poor attempts to mask vices with the characteristics of virtue. The posts seek recognition and importance that are contrary to virtue. What we must come to understand is that true virtue does not seek reward or recognition of character, but instead is simply done without importance to self.

Just as a coin has two opposite sides, each Vice has a Virtue to balance it. Virtue is defined as the quality of being morally good and the sense of moral excellence. More so, personal virtues are characteristics valued as promoting collective and individual greatness. Every religion, philosophy, and culture have a variation of what they consider as virtues. The virtues I will use are the ones found in Christian-Judea doctrine; and are the antipodal of the Vices from the last chapter. The seven Virtues are, Chastity, Temperance, Charity, Humility, Patience, Kindness, and Diligence.

Chastity is often times associated with sexual abstinence but Chastity is more than that. Simply put it is Purity of heart. Purity born of vestal thoughts and the absence of malice.

Temperance or Self-Control is the measured forbearance of one's actions. It is the constraint to partake just enough and give the surplus to those who are in need. In doing so, it also is the gateway to the next Virtue of Charity.

Charity is not just about giving onto others. It is giving onto others <u>more</u> than what you would give yourself. Charity is putting the physical needs of others before your own.

Humility is quality of being humble regardless of situation or achievement. Greatness exhibiting meekness is the epitome of Humility. It does not seek praise or reward; it does not seek elevation of status.

Patience is the capacity to endure and demonstrate composure especially in the most adverse of conditions. A person with patience will not let anger control them, even in the presence of anger.

Kindness is similar to Charity that what is given is not physical but more emotional and spiritual. Kindness seeks to give and provide for selfless reasons, while Envy seeks to take for selfish reasons.

Diligence is a vigor or intensity of action. It provides purpose and seeks to growth. In most cases, Diligence's higher purpose creates benefits and prosperity to more than one's self – it provides for the greater good.

These Virtues represent the best of humanity's given characteristics. While Vices are more attuned to desires of the physical world, Virtues feed our spiritual needs. Some say these Virtues is how we know we have souls, as it is our soul that requires the nourishment from the bounty of virtues. "Fulfilling a Virtue is more rewarding than fulfilling a Vice for two reasons. One, it is inherently challenging to accomplish a surpassing act of goodness in a world that's rife with selfishness and aggression. Doing so demands sacrifice and perseverance. Two, the temptation to indulge base inclinations and desires is constant and often means taking the path of least resistance, which precludes doing the greater good. Fulfilling Vices therefore offers small rewards that are easy to come by." (White Wolf Publishing)

To exhibit and practice these virtues is never an easy task. It requires a strong will and consistent selfless thought. In Arthurian legend, even the most devote Knight, Lancelot could not uphold his virtues and instead fell to his vices. It definitely is a constant battle to be fought within ourselves. The rivalry of vice against virtue have been apparent throughout history. A Latin poet named Prudentius wrote Psychomachia; a story in which portrays a battle for the soul of man between Vices and Virtues. In the poem the Virtues eventually defeats the Vices; however, we know that is not always the case on our own personal accounts. Too easily do humans fall victim to the Vices and forget the Virtues. Just as in everything in life, it is the choices we make and the paths we travel on whether or not our Vices or Virtues prevail.

"Virtues are acquired through endeavor, which rests wholly upon yourself."
--Sidney Lanier

A Journey of Insights

CHAPTER SEVENTEEN

Warrior Soul, Poet Heart

"All of the significant battles are waged within the self."
--Sheldon Kopp

The wet bulb index read a blistering 90 with the unforgiving Kentucky humidity. Sweat poured from my brow as the sun beat down on my Kevlar helmet. My uniform was completely drenched and my battle gear seem to weigh like a ton. Our bayonets were fixed atop of our M16A2 rifles. The sand filled dummies stood in front of each soldier, as we stared with anticipation.

Suddenly a load bellow called out, "What makes the grass grow green?"

We thundered in return, "Blood! Blood makes the grass grow green!"

The response was not adequate, "What makes the grass grow greener?" "

We responded once again, "Guts! Guts make the grass grow greener Drill Sergeant!"

Words that I will never forget as it was ingrained into my mind during my training in the military. I never understood modern warriorship. It heckled gentleness and humility but idolized boastfulness and violence. True, that the latter characteristics are requisites in an efficient soldier, but the former are what soldiers need to preserve their souls. I mentioned that we are constantly faced with battles that wage within our inner selves. We are all natural fighters inside; and this is apparent with our survival instincts, our perseverance, and beliefs. As much as we are innate warriors, we are also poets deep in our hearts. Through music, art, and expression we exhibit the poet in us. This duality of warrior and poet is natural paradox within humanity. We seek peace and love yet we are quick to wage war and fight for our beliefs.

To have the soul of a warrior does not necessarily mean to be combative nor does it fully apply to the physical world. The warrior's soul is rooted deep within our hearts, minds, and spirits. The wars waged in the physical world are important for natural survival, but it is the inner ones that determine the final outcome of our own humanity. And in doing so, it also determines the final fate of our species. The wars within our hearts are never resolved and are always at siege by despair, hate, and treachery. All the vices are constantly knocking at the gates of our soul. It is important to embrace the natural warrior in you as it is this warrior soul that gives you mettle and dauntlessness. The manifestation of physical strength is a direct correlation of the strength measured in your soul. The relentless ability to refuse surrender and the fortitude to be steadfast in face of hopelessness is the hallmark of our warrior spirit. The elements that forges a complete warrior, must come from within.

Having a warrior's soul is indeed both a desirable and admirable attribute, but it is the poets heart that provides the inspiration to achieve, and the intonation for love. Being a poet means more than just being able to compose captivating phrases on paper. A poet looks at the world with uncovered eyes. A poet can see wrong and dream of ways to make them right. A poet sees beauty in things where others only see distortion. A poet can distinguish between the superficial and the profound. Where the warrior's soul provides strength, courage, and perseverance, the poet's heart imbues with serenity, grace, and artistry. In serenity the poet finds wisdom; in grace he finds compassion; and in artistry he finds the canvass of expression. The poet's pen is as strong as his sword – and many times his words can reach far many more than his blade.

Most people tend to favor one side more than the other. And most people would think one side may be too cruel or too weak. The reality is that both is necessary to achieve a better understanding of the world. In these modern times, it is a rarity to find someone that truly balances their warriorship and poet. The times of Paladins, Samurais, and Greek soldiers are all but gone. That does not mean however, it cannot be achieved today nor should we stop striving for it. Accomplishing this balance is an incredible feat, that reveals new life perspectives. Heaven and Earth becomes a singularity rather than separate concepts. It brings clarity to the universe and a step closer to enlightenment. Above all it will allow you to see with your eyes and feel with your heart, while being the strength for those around you.

"The challenge of warriorship is to step out into space, by being brave and at the same time gentle."
--Chogyam Trungpa

CHAPTER EIGHTEEN

Copper Over Gold

"A person starts to live when he can live outside of himself."
--Albert Einstein

Even though I would not call myself religious by any standard, Catholicism played a huge part of my life as a child. Every Sunday, our family went to mass, and every Sunday I was an Altar Boy, specifically the cross bearer. Bible School in the summer was mandatory for me so we studied a lot of the Bible's parables and wisdom. One passage from the Book of Mark that still sits with me is called The Widow's Offering, and it goes like this:

Jesus sat down opposite the place where the offerings were put and watched the crowd putting their money into the temple treasury. Many rich people threw in large amounts. But a poor widow came and put in two very small copper coins, worth only a few cents. Calling his disciples to him, Jesus said, "Truly I tell you, this poor widow has put more into the treasury than all the others. They all gave out of their wealth; but she, out of her poverty, put in everything—all she had to live on."

On the surface gold will always be more valuable than copper. But sometimes value is not defined by its materiality, but by its relative intent. The value of our actions is measured on the value we hold for that action. In other words, value is not absolute, but relative to the holder. In the parable, the widow's copper was worth more to her, than the gold was worth to rich people. It was easy for the rich to give which they had plenty of, and she gave all she had. There is another lesson in the parable as well. That lesson is, beware of generosity cloaked with ulterior motives. Though the rich people seem to be generous and giving for selfless reasons, they were actually giving for selfish reasons. They flaunted their gold, and their generosity was born of brandish boastfulness. The rich wanted to show how much they gave, so that they may be revered and honored by others. But it was the widow whose intent was pure benevolence as she sacrificially gave from her heart, whereas the man gave to show off his wealth.

These lessons of the parable should always be remembered in our daily lives. These principles strictly stem from the heart and sacrifice to the service of others. To put others above oneself is to demonstrate the virtues of Charity and Kindness. I will acknowledge that no matter how noble these principles are; it is definitely not an easy feat to follow them. No one is expecting you to be devoutly pious and immolate your life to nothingness – however you should expect yourself to act with the kindness and charity you would expect of others. "People have this idea that the more pious and devout I am, the more successful I am. Which is very dangerous. If you look at faith in that way, you're bound to fail at both - spiritually and in your career" (Troy Polamalu).

To be perfectly honest, I did not know why I even wrote this chapter in the book, and I could not find the heart to remove it. One day, it finally came to me – I wrote this chapter as a reminder to myself to always try to be kind and charitable. Most importantly, it was a reminder to myself to make an impact to the world when I can. I am definitely not a rich man, but I do well enough for myself. I have my fair share of problems and struggles, but for the little time I have on this Earth, I can try to be an example. An example to my daughters, my friends, my family, and my fellow man. Maybe it is just the ghosts of my guilt that I am trying to appease through these acts of generosity and kindness. Whatever the reason, these are lessons I that still believe in, and maybe one day, God willing, I will become a better man for those around me.

"Mankind's role is to fulfill his heaven-sent purpose through a sincere heart that is in harmony with all creation and loves all things."
--Morihei Ueshiba

CHAPTER NINETEEN

Perfect Imperfections

"We in our own human imperfections are repelled by the perfect, since everything is apparent from the start and there is no suggestion of the infinite."
--Soetsu Yanagi

Being of Filipino descent, an Asian culture, it was not uncommon for my parents to expect perfection. Nothing less than straight A's on the report card was acceptable. You had to be the model student, exceling in everything to include perfect attendance. There is even a joke about an Asian "F" is an "A minus" on your report card. Though these expectations sound marvelous on the surface, they are actually very detrimental to an impressionable child trying to find their own identity in the world. Expectations is one thing, but forcing perfection is never a good message to send a child.

In many cultures deliberate imperfections are integrated into their daily lives. For example, in the Navajo rug, there is always one clear imperfection that is woven into the tapestry. The process of the manual weaving is time consuming and every part is carefully considered – since it is such a laborious task, the Navajo believed part of their spirit is integrated into the rug. The one imperfection in the rug is called "the spirit string", and where the spirit moves in and out of the rug. The imperfection is subtle but symbolizes our humanity. This deliberate imperfection also exists in Islamic art, Persian rugs, Greek sculptures, Amish quilts, Turkish ships, Orthodox Jewish houses and Japanese Zen ceramics. The Japanese called this philosophy Wabi Sabi in which aesthetics and a world view is centered on the acceptance of transience and imperfection. The aesthetic is sometimes described as one of beauty that is "imperfect, impermanent, and incomplete". This philosophy is consistent that everything in the universe is always changing and transient, so achieving any type of perfection would be impossible anyways. Accepting imperfections is not about accepting mediocrity and carelessness, it is about appreciating the natural state of the universe. For example, every snowflake has a complete pattern than the next – so who is to say that one snowflake is flawed and the other is perfect – they are simply different.

In a world where perfection is greatly admired, it is simple to lose sight that as human beings, we are not born perfect, nor can we achieve that label in any fashion. Trying to achieve perfection is to condemn yourself to a life of sadness and misery. Indeed, if anyone were able to reach perfection, then life would no longer be challenging or interesting; and would become stagnant and learning would. But as fate would have it, life is never perfect. Lucky for us life is full of surprises.

Part of self-realization is knowing that you are not perfect and you are bound to make mistakes. Accepting yourself for your flaws and shortcomings does not mean that you should not try to improve yourself. It simply means understanding who you are and your limitations. On the contrary, you should always attempt to better yourself, but never losing sight that perfection is not a human quality. Everyone will make mistakes and those mistakes can be painful and soul wrecking. A mistake is only bad if a lesson is not learned from it, but fortunately we do learn from the mistakes. Be happy with whom you are and with what you have, but always strive to make things better for yourself. Continue to grow and learn from life. Living a full and happy life goes hand in hand with knowing that perfection is not the goal; but doing the best you can with what you have. Despite the limits set upon us by our own humanity, the challenge of striving for something better, is always before us. Never let the things you can't do interfere with what you can do. The simple belief that you can achieve dreams will give you the inspiration. There will be people in your life journey that you will meet, who "seem perfect" in all they do, but that is just a perception. Those same people are merely doing their best with what they have been given – playing the hand they have been dealt. As a parent myself, hopefully I have learned not to impose perfection on my children, but to impart the beauty of imperfections.

"Accepting the world as imperfect, unfinished, and transient, and then going deeper and celebrating that reality, is something not unlike freedom."
--Richard Powell

CHAPTER TWENTY

Destination Unknown

"You cannot change your destination overnight, but you can change your direction overnight."
--Jim Rohn

Since I started this book over sixteen years ago, I have always been searching for answers in my life. And I thought with age, I would be wiser and eventually have all the answers I would seek. Instead, for every answer I found, many more new questions arose. Life has definitely been interesting and eventful. Some accomplishments I am proud of, and yet other failures, I am covered in shame. I am pretty sure that you too have felt that the problems of the world seem unsolvable? And that any decision you make will have a wrong outcome – and where no one wins and everyone loses. It is not uncommon that life will throw you into a situation so complicated that there will be no definitive answer or apparent solution to the problem.

There will be times that making a decision is the problem itself – and the worst part is you have to make a decision. Because we cannot see in the future nor can we determine the long term outcome, we will be overwhelmed with feelings of doubt, insecurity, and hesitation which leads to the procrastination of making this life altering decision.

When faced with this dilemma, there are only two options that you can do. The first is not to make any decision at all – to simply wait and let time decide for you. By not making a decision, you are actually letting time and circumstance make the choice for you. It is a passive way of allowing the future to materialize without directly influencing the outcome. This passive decision making takes very little energy on our part and follows the path of least resistance. When faced with tough decisions, most people opt to use the 'do-nothing' approach. True, this is the easiest, but the problem is that it may yield the least desirable results.

The second option is to take the bold stance and actually make a conscious choice between two paths. When making a conscious decision, you are actually committing to a path. This takes a lot of energy and involves a lot of effort and thought. It weighs out the pros and cons, and an attempt to narrow down to the best possible solution. Because we have so many paths to travel and so many decisions to make, it is absolutely inevitable that we will make bad choices. However, do remember for your sake and the sake of others that bad choices does not necessarily equate to a bad person. No matter the outcome, these conscious decisions are the best reflections of our souls. Freewill is a gift, but also a curse. In freewill, we will find the best and worst versions of ourselves.

There have been many times in my life when I am overcome with complete helplessness as I don't have the answers I seek. I have to remind myself that it is natural and alright to feel this way; and that I cannot lose faith, hope, or your heart. Sometimes you just have let things be, even though it is the hardest thing to do. A great part of living is not having the right answers. We are all searching for the answers of our lives. Though we are all different in many ways, we all search for the same solutions to life, love, and happiness. We all have laid awake at night staring into the darkness in deep contemplation. With every heartbeat each second passes, and we struggle to find an answer. It is very frustrating and scary not knowing what the future holds for each of us, but that is what makes life so interesting and mystifying.

The road less traveled strikes fear and doubt in many hearts. The feeling of unknowing prevents many from making a final decision. Taking the necessary risks is definitely not an easy matter. It takes great courage and faith to make changes in your life. When we are comfortable in one situation, it is difficult to sail away to uncharted oceans. When you stay with comfort then you will never know what adventures may lie ahead. The universe is a series of cause and effects, but also a series of 'random' occurrences. Though destiny plays a part in the overall scheme, our daily lives are filled with chance encounters. True, I said that there are no coincidences, and I still hold that belief. The actual event itself is predestined, the type of event is where the randomness occurs. Think of it this way: It is like picking a lottery ball. The act of picking up the ball itself is not random, but the actual number resulting from that action is. Bottom line is no matter how much you search for an answer in some matters of life, there will be no clear solution. No matter the path you travel, may faith, love, and destiny be always with you on your journey of life.

"Follow what you are genuinely passionate about and let that guide you to your destination."
--Diane Sawyer

CHAPTER TWENTY-ONE

Universal Truths

"Happiness cannot be traveled to, owned, earned, or worn. It is the spiritual experience of living every minute with love, grace & gratitude."
--Denis Waitley

There is no written universal law that says good men will always triumph over evil. Nor does it say that evil will fail in the opposition of good. Nature does not take sides, or delineate between good or evil. The matter of fact is, that life simply happens. We cannot expect that the universe will always reward the just and punish the wicked. As it stands, it rarely happens in that fashion. We cannot control the events that are set before our paths, but we can control the way we react to them. And even more importantly we can choose how we live. There are a few golden rules that I try to live by - simple to understand but difficult to follow.

<u>Everything is a Choice</u>. It is very easy to put blame on others and especially placing blame on circumstance. The truth is that all the major aspects of your life was based on a choice. Your career, your love life, the way you dress, lifestyle, friends, and even the way you feel today are results of choices. We must understand that we hold power over ourselves, and the actions to become who we want to be. Every day we are given the opportunity to be a better person; to exhibit kindness, compassion, temperance, and humility, or we can choose anger, hatred, indifference, and selfishness. The moment we realize the we are not victims, but are the owners of our actions that can lead to a better life, then that is the moment of empowerment.

<u>Happiness Comes from Within</u>. "Happiness cannot be traveled to, owned, earned, worn, or consumed. Happiness is the spiritual experience of living every minute with love, grace, and gratitude" (Denis Waitley). We truly own the key to our contentment, as misery is not determined by circumstance but by our disposition. Too often we look at others and feel unhappy for our lacking. There are people in the world that have very little yet are very happy with their lives. On the contrast, there are those with everything they ever wanted, and

yet are never content. True happiness comes from within and is a choice to be made. Happiness is not determined by the best circumstance or defined by optimal conditions. Happiness is a choice and the ability be grateful despite less than favorable conditions. You are solely responsible for your disposition and attitude. Even in the midst of misery, you can determine your own happiness.

Everything Changes. Nothing in the universe is immune to change. Life is constantly evolving, expanding, and even deteriorating. Neither progress nor achievement is impossible without change. It is the vehicle in which all life moves forward. Change can occur like a violent storm and have immediate impacts, or it can come subtly like a summer breeze. Even our very thoughts are susceptible with every turn in our journey. Our views of the world, and the way we interact with it changes through the years, as we grow with experience and wisdom. To understand this is to know a universal truth. And with this truth comes acceptance to flow and move with the universe.

Time Heals and Tells All. Another constant beyond death is time. Through time, the past becomes distant memories, and may be even forgotten. Time is the mender of hearts and the oracle of the future. In the moments we live in, we never see the purpose that is to come nor do we comprehend the reasons behind them. Only when we look back do we realize both purpose and reason. In its own eventuality, time answers all questions and reveals what is meant to be. And through time, both pain and joy become simply a part of our own history. It soothes us a little at a time, until we no longer feel the pain; and all that are left are lessons. On the opposite spectrum, time reinforces and sustains our joys through memories.

<u>Live Life</u>. Life is full of wonders and opportunities but also full of uncertainty and fear. As I mentioned before, having no fear can be detrimental, but living in fear is definitely debilitating. When we let fear dictate our actions, then we become so cautious and forget to take risks - and without risks, there are no rewards. You should know however that there is a fundamental difference between living recklessly and living with risk. Reckless living is to act absolutely without thought to consequence. Taking risks is to understand the worth and value of the possibility, while reducing the negative impacts. You must remember that every breath of your life is to be cherished, but at the same time, we do not

have infinite moments to live out your dreams. Life will be both difficult and rich; there will be heartbreaks, pain, joy, laughter, tears, wonder, disappointment, but most importantly there will be love. The days ahead of you are yet to come, and each moment waiting to be greeted and embraced. We may not be able to determine how we die, but we can certainly choose how we live. "Don't be afraid of Dying; Be afraid of Not Living." (unknown)

"I think you find universal truth when you get really honest with yourself and you can reach people. If you go deep enough, you have that core feeling, and that feeling can transcend the details of your experience".
--Rachel Platten

CHAPTER TWENTY-TWO

In Solitude We Hear

"The best advice you give, is the one you follow yourself"
--Elm Valle

While you read this book, I sincerely hope that you do not get the impression that I am preaching. To preach wisdom is simple, but to act on your own advice is difficult. Even more difficult is to listen to the wisdom of others and follow them. To listen and hear wisdom is sensible and insightful. To put those words, dreams, or ideas into action is the foundation of greatness. George Gordon Byron once said that "In Solitude, where we are least alone." What Byron meant by those words is that when we left alone in silence, is when our thoughts come to haunt us. The solitude of silence becomes ear deafening as our minds race, replaying moments, hours, days, weeks, and even years. Silence is always where we contemplate the deepest and learn the most about ourselves and the world. Unfortunately, our lives are hectic and those moments of solitude are far and few. We consistently forget and fail to contemplate and meditate on wisdom from the past. And sometimes saying nothing, is better than saying anything at all. As we approach close to the end of this book, I wanted to just give you some quotes to reflect on, and hopefully you can use them sometime in your future. It may change your life, then again it may not – but what is important is that you understand how to apply it to your own life.

"If you want to be happy, be."
--Henry David Thoreau

"May you live all the days of your life."
--Jonathan Swift

"Education is not filling a bucket, but lighting a fire."
--William Butler Yeats

"Personally, I am always ready to learn, although I do not always like being taught"
--Winston Churchill

"To know others is wisdom, to know oneself is enlightenment."
--Tao Te Ching

"Words that come from the heart enter the heart."
--Sages

"One touch of nature makes the whole world kin."
--Shakespeare
"The Journey is the reward."
--Tao saying

"Make voyages. Attempt them. There's nothing else."
 --Tennessee Williams

"If you are to be, you must begin by assuming
responsibility."
--Richard Bach

"The more you depend on forces outside of yourself, the
more you are dominated by them."
 --Unknown

"All suffering prepares the soul for vision."
 --Martin Buber

"There is no greatness where there is no simplicity,
goodness, and truth."
--Leo Tolstoy

"It's never too late to have a happy childhood."
--Unknown

"When one door of happiness closes, another one opens.
But often we look so long at the closed door that we do
not see that one that has been opened for us."
--Helen Keller--

"We are the living links in a life force that moves and
plays through and around us, binding the deepest soils
with the farthest stars."
--Alan Chadwick--

"Every moment of your life is infinitely creative and the
universe is endlessly bountiful. Just put forth a clear

enough request, and everything your heart desires must come to you."
--Shakti Gawain

"Man cannot discover new oceans until he has courage to lose sight of the shore."
--Unknown—

"Resolve to be tender with the young, compassionate with the aged, sympathetic with striving, and tolerant with the weak and the wrong. Sometime in life you will have been all of these."
--Lloyd Sheare

"If we could read the secret history of our enemies, we would find in each man's life a sorrow and a suffering enough to disarm all hostility."
--Henry Wadsworth Longfellow

"Don't be afraid to be weak.
Don't be too proud to be strong.
Just open up your heart my friend...
If you want, then start to cry
If you can, then start to laugh
Just believe in Destiny..."
--Enya

"Art, Music, Language. All but expressions of the greatest asset the human race has: The Human Soul."
--E. C. Valle

CHAPTER TWENTY-THREE

Departing Thoughts

"Promise to yourself to be so strong that nothing can disturb your peace of mind. To be too wise for worry, too tolerant for anger, and too courageous for fear. To Be Happy."
-- Unknown

     Well I have finally come to finish this book. The journey was definitely long and arduous, but nonetheless a satisfying one. I never thought I would finish this as the years gone by, so did my perspective on life and consequently, this book as well. As you come to the end of your journey of reading this book, realize that there will be many more journeys ahead of you. Life will offer you both wonderful and miserable experiences. You *will* find answers to some questions and yet many dilemmas will go unsolved. The wisdom you learn during your lifetime will be valuable to prosperity. Teach your friends and learn from your enemies. Practice kindness and establish compassion.

Live in every moment and keep your senses sharp. You will fail at many things, but rest assured you will also succeed in many more.

The universe is so large and infinite that we will not be able to understand everything. The things you see will shape and mold your perceptions, but never let the things you don't see, pass you by. Believe in faith. Keep courage close to your heart because you will need it. Understand fear and how it affects you, because that will also help you in your life. Reflect - It is a great way to keep sane and keep in touch with your soul.

I never promised answers but only insights and advice. To be human is to make errors, as long as you learn from them. I hope that you have learned something from this book. I hope that you are little wiser, smarter, and a little more open to the world. It is not about winning, or having the fastest car, or even having the best job. It is about doing your best; for yourself, others, and the world. Pain is inevitable, but so is joy. Life is a tragedy, a comedy, and a romance; the kind you live is up to you. Happiness cannot be sought, bought, or owned, it can only be realized.

Realize your strengths, weaknesses, and potential. You are a unique individual that is part of the whole universe. Your actions affect everything else in the universe. You are part of the cosmic puzzle. Without you the picture is not complete, and without the rest, you are not complete. Share with others your thoughts and feelings for they are the gateways to your heart. Break the boundaries around you. Feel free and be free; in mind, spirit, and heart. Seriousness is essential, but if you are serious all the time, you will not be able to dream. Dream as if you were a child, and pursue those dreams with the conviction of a wise adult.

The world can be a mystifying and wondrous place, if you look hard enough. The rain will fall and the sky will cast dark clouds over you. If it was always sunny, the world would become a desert. Your life is up to you. Life provides the canvas; you do the painting. As you come to close this book, remember the words within these pages, and promise me one thing: Live a life worth remembering!

"'Your task...to build a better world,' God said. I answered, 'How? ... this world is such a large, vast place, and there's nothing I do.' But God in all His wisdom said, 'just build a better you.'"
--Unknown

A Journey of Insights

❧

Afterthought

Completing this book was definitely a huge achievement for me. In the past two decades, every time I picked it up to write again, I changed chapters, thoughts, and ideas. It showed how much I have changed over time. Life for me has been more than interesting with many of ups and downs. I know this book is far from the great American novel and definitely far from perfect, but nonetheless, it is something I am proud of. Just like the Navajo rug, the imperfections found in this book symbolizes the pureness of my ideas and the flow of my thoughts. Hopefully the little bits of insights and wisdom written within these pages are enough to inspire you to always have Hope and Dreams; and to always be the best version of yourself, no matter how difficult life may be. And to never give up despite circumstance or obstacles. Lastly, I always want you to remember, to always keep an open heart, and always have room for love. Thank you for reading this – I will always be grateful that I was able to share a part of me with you!

A Journey of Insights

ABOUT THE AUTHOR

Elm Valle is a US Army Veteran with a Bachelors in Psychology from the University of California at Davis and a Master's in Administration from Central Michigan University. Elm is currently working as a Global Supply Chain Director and is a subject matter expert speaker in his profession. His travels have taken him to places like Rome, Berchtesgaden, Luxembourg, Rio de Janeiro, Amsterdam, and many more places. Living in various countries outside the United States, Elm, learned to experience firsthand the wonders, achievements, cuisines, and philosophies of various cultures. Elm's affinity and passion for the mysteries of life is apparent and is always active. He has done competitive bodybuilding, play guitar and piano, scuba-diving, rappelling, motorcycling, and of course writing. Elm is also a father to two wonderful daughters.

A Journey of Insights

Soul Ascension

A Journey of Insights

By
Elm Valle

Made in the USA
Middletown, DE
02 August 2016